The
Eighteen Absent Years of Jesus Christ

by
Lloyd Kenyon Jones

Illustrations from the Old Masters

THE BOOK TREE
San Diego, California

Originally published
1943
by The Kaden Publishing Co.
Chicago

New material, revisions and cover
© 2006
The Book Tree

ISBN 978-1-58509-271-0

Published by
The Book Tree
P.O. Box 16476
San Diego, CA 92176
www.thebooktree.com

We provide fascinating and educational products to help awaken the public to new ideas and
information that would not be available otherwise.
Call 1 (800) 700-8733 for our *FREE BOOK TREE CATALOG*.

CHRIST AT THE BEGINNING OF THE "ABSENT YEARS"

THE 18 ABSENT YEARS OF JESUS CHRIST

CONTENTS

ILLUSTRATIONS

PREFACE

Where was Jesus between the ages of 12 and 30? The Bible says nothing of these years or his whereabouts during that time. There are clues, however, and the author follows some of them in this book, bringing us to a conclusion which he feels is the most obvious. It's been claimed that there have been more books written on the subject of Jesus than on any other subject in the history of publishing. There have been so many books over the years that put forth so many different theories about Jesus - that he was married, that he survived the crucifixion, that he came from outer space, that he was an Essene, that he founded Mormonism, that he traveled to India, to Egypt, to Tibet, to South and Central America, and a host of other ideas that are sometimes probable, but more often stand as nothing more than conjecture. So what happened during the "lost years of Jesus"? Jones presents here a very simple and rational solution that could in fact make more sense than all the other theories combined. Chapter titles include The Improbable Journey into Thibet; The Family of Jesus; Jesus, the Worker in Wood; Christ's Power of Healing; The Education of Jesus; and To Those Who Would Follow in the Way He Led.

Paul Tice

FOREWORD

Lloyd Kenyon Jones, like many other writers, got his first taste of newspaper work by filling the job of "printer's devil" in his home town. Then, later, like most ambitious men, he worked for many newspapers in larger cities.

Lloyd Kenyon Jones read extensively, his mind having a leaning toward the mystical and the occult.

At one time he practiced hypnotism and toured the country giving performances of his powers as a mind reader and hypnotist. His feature stunt was to drive a team of horses down the street—blindfolded, and stop at a given point and there find a hidden object—blindfolded.

Later, he returned to private life to begin a study of East Indian Yogi and Buddhism and Spiritualism, — mystical and occult studies and research, subjects always so dear to his heart.

He found to his satisfaction, after years of study on these subjects, that the Bible is the true guide, and his remaining years were spent as a scholar.

THE 18 ABSENT YEARS OF JESUS CHRIST

Not unlike the great scholar Bergson, who studied Greek and Oriental mysticism and the Prophets of Israel, and who said he believed that Christian Mysticism is the "only one which has truly come to fruition", Mr. Jones states in his book that "The Yogis and other Eastern leaders cloak their meanings in mysterious terms."

Lloyd Kenyon Jones was a sincere Bible student and in order to spread the results of his searchings for the Truth, — he wrote this book, The Eighteen "Absent Years" of Jesus Christ, which is now published as a posthumous work which Mr. Jones had completed at the time of his death.

Upon a thorough reading of this volume, the reader will feel impelled with a higher knowledge and clearer idealism of a more constructive path of Bible information which this book purports to give, no matter what your age may be, your beliefs, or what your previous reading studies may have taught you.

The illustrations in this book are reproductions of the Old Masters.

INTRODUCTION

What was the life of Jesus Christ from the age of twelve until the age of thirty? For all these centuries, people have puzzled over this period. Books have been written on the subject and any student of the Scriptures will find it fascinating to trace the different clues.

From the time that the Boy of twelve confounded the doctors in the Temple, when He was missing for three days, until His Baptism by John, there is little in the New Testament to indicate His whereabouts.

Jesus Christ was and is the most tragic and majestic figure in all history. Yet for some years after His birth, He and His parents remained hidden in Egypt lest the Child be slain. And so swift were the events following His public appearance and works, terminating in the Crucifixion, it would appear that these missing eighteen years should have been of profound and even tremendous importance. In fact, they were.

THE 18 ABSENT YEARS OF JESUS CHRIST

The God-Man during those hidden years gave no sign which history records of His great powers. He had them always but they remained dormant because "His time had not yet come." There are many theories about His unrecorded life. Let us consider some of them.

There is a theory that Christ, while a boy, went to Thibet to study with the sages of that country. We will discuss that in our first chapter.

He lived at Nazareth for many years, in fact, until the beginning of His Public Life. During that Public Life, He performed miracles, preached and gave us the New Law in its entirety. Did He grow up from childhood as does an ordinary boy? Had He a home on this earth and an earthly father and mother?

The Scriptures answer all these questions and, in the following pages, you will find a discussion of them.

THE 18 ABSENT YEARS OF JESUS CHRIST

CHAPTER I

The Improbable Journey into Thibet

The historians who endeavor to prove that Christ, when in His early teens, journeyed farther into the Orient disregard the words of the Scripture on which any authentic thinking must be based. We are told that His father, Joseph, was told by an angel in a dream to take the Child and His mother into Egypt to escape the murderous designs of King Herod, after the visit of the Wise Men. "Arise and take the child and his mother and flee into Egypt; and remain there until I tell thee. For Herod will seek the child to destroy him." After Herod's death, another angel appeared to announce that they might return. As Herod died, approximately, about 2 A.D., the Child was still only a baby when they made the journey to Galilee, to the town of Nazareth. And after His visit to the Temple, we are told, Christ returned to their home with His father and mother, "and was subject to them."

There is no further history of that life at

—The Flight into Egypt...

Nazareth beyond the fact that "He grew in age and in wisdom."

His intelligence grew naturally with the other qualities of His humanity; the fact that His wisdom "astonished" the rabbis and the high-priests proves that He had no need to study in far lands to know the truth. He was "the Word of God made flesh." He had the truth: He was Eternal Truth become man; He had no need to seek for it.

And in His public life, He spoke in no ambiguous language but in parables such as a practical man would use. His message was clothed in language not difficult to understand, whereas the Yogis and other Eastern religious leaders cloak their meanings in mysterious terms.

Christ used simple, homely things for illustrating His meanings; He spoke to the multitudes in words which they could understand; words which have been translated into all tongues and can be understood by all peoples and in all times.

These parables and sermons are as easily applied to the every day life of today as they were then. We read the verse, "Not a sparrow falls," and find consolation in the words.

The Old Testament had been written down on parchment and vellum, fastened to rolls and furled as scrolls. Whether Christ had access to these "books" of the Old Testament is not known. He learned, as any other child, from His mother and father. His Mother, Mary, had been offered to the Temple at the age of three and remained there until her betrothal to Joseph. Among the other duties required of the maidens, a profound study of the Scriptures was important. Mary is supposed to have been wedded to Joseph at the age of fifteen, which was maturity in that day and in that country. In all those years she must have learned much which she imparted to her little Son as He "grew in age and in wisdom."

Certainly she taught Him His prayers, as the mother of today teaches her little ones, for Mary prayed often to God Who was the real Father of the Child.

There were religions which did not come
from Revelation. The religion of Persia, which
was founded on Zoroaster's teachings, and em-
bodied the Zend-Avesta. Then, too, there were
those writings and teachings which guided the
ancient Egyptians in their religious belief, known
as the Book of the Dead. That magical and mystical collection had widespread power throughout the Levant and the Orient.

There were other religions, many of them
consisting of sun-worship and fire-worship. They
were entirely pagan.

Undoubtedly Christ knew of them and their
falsity. Tales were told by travellers and by
merchants who went to other lands for the goods
which they sold in the market-place in the towns
and villages. Or perhaps priests of these strange
rites and occult practices came into Galilee to
try to induce the Jews to follow them. Even had
Christ not been graced with wisdom beyond the

ordinary child, He would have heard and thought about these strange cults which did not come from His "Father Who art in Heaven." He had no need to study them but knew about them for He referred to false religions in his sermons and teachings. "The Child grew and became strong. He was full of wisdom and the grace of God was upon Him."

We can picture the gracious and lovely Boy with his mother and father, gathered with the other villagers, seated about some travellers from the East who told them strange tales of those peoples. The Child's eyes, perhaps, clouded with pity when he heard of the strange rites and pagan customs of those who knew not His Father. Some day, the Truth would be brought to these peoples and to the farthest corners of the world! Perhaps He pondered on it as He walked home in the soft blue twilight confidingly hand in hand with Mary and Joseph; perhaps He spoke then of His love for all men. His mother had been told, at His circumcision, of a sword which would pierce her heart. Did she hold His little hand the tighter, knowing

16

that, one day, that universal love of His would bring desolation to her heart?

And, doubtless, the synagogue which He attended had scrolls of the Holy Writ. If the Child was not permitted to study them Himself, they were read aloud and explained by the rabbi. For Joseph and his family attended the synagogue every Sabbath and on the great feasts as prescribed by the Jewish law. Until the coming of the New Law, which Jesus Christ himself was to establish on earth, God had given His rules to Moses for the Jews to obey in the Ten Commandments. His only Son would be certain to obey them. And "Joseph was a just man." He and Mary, who were always obedient to the Will of the Most High, certainly would fulfill that obligation. Once a year they went to Jerusalem for the Pasch. The Child heard the learned and the holy expound the Scriptures. So, in a natural way, he "grew in wisdom" as Luke states.

Had Jesus been free to spend all His time in studying, and had He the money to travel to carry on research, then we might speculate as to whether His eighteen unaccounted-for years had been devoted to study the religions of other lands: had it been a necessary part of His "Father's business," He would have done so. He knew His Father's will; that He, Himself, was to found the true religion; that He, Himself, was to be its High-priest and Victim. There was no need for Him to go far afield. The Truth was in the little house at Nazareth although the time had not yet come for that truth to be known.

But Jesus was not only divine; He was also human and He had that to do which all the angels and the archangels could not accomplish. But first He chose to live with mankind as a man Himself, to feel the pinch of poverty, to "earn His bread by the sweat of His brow;" to live the humble life of a peasant in a humble village.

He knew His destiny. He came into the world knowing it. In the Epistle to the Hebrews, it says that "entering into the world, He said, Behold I come. In the head of the book it is written of me that I should do Thy will, O God." We know that His mother knew it also, for she "pondered all these things in her heart." From the time of the Annunciation, she knew that she was to be the mother of God. At the time of the Nativity, she knew that the little helpless infant whom she cradled in her loving arms had come for the salvation of man. And she knew the prophecies which foretold the sufferings and death of the Messiah, "the most despised and rejected of men." There is a famous picture of the mother watching Joseph and his Foster-Son at work as carpenters. The little Boy has lifted a cross-beam of wood from the floor of the shop; the mother, with her work fallen to her lap, looks at him with troubled eyes. It is the habit of mothers to plan for their sons' futures. Will he be great? Will he be powerful? This mother knew that while her Son would be both great and powerful it would be accomplished only by suffering such as no man before or since has endured, suffering of both mind and body and for the good of ungrateful man. For many do not want to know Him or prefer to persist in their sins. They see only the greatness of riches. But Christ's power and greatness are of the greater world of Eternity.

Whether Mary imparted this knowledge to her Son or whether He knew it by Divine inspiration, we know that by the time He was twelve and they went up to the Temple at Jerusalem He was conscious of His destiny; that He was the Son of God made man. The loving and obedient Son had obeyed a higher call; He was "about His Father's business."

So He knew the prophecies and that He was to be the Victim and Sacrifice to atone for the sins of man. We are told that He was the perfect man. He had, innately, all the moral and physical virtues, which developed as He grew from infancy to boyhood and then to young manhood. Bravery is a high quality of the soul and heart. Great bravery has been shown in the war by our own boys and we are proud of their spirit. Yet was there ever bravery to compare with that of the Boy who, reading the Prophecies, knew that they foretold His own suffering and death? He did not roll up the scroll and flee from the terrible words but read on and on, knowing surely that it would all come to pass and that, when He grew to manhood, He would have to endure it all! "Greater love than this no man hath; than he should lay down his life for his friend."

Love was His inspiration; first, His love for His Heavenly Father whose Justice must be appeased. He loved His mother and His earthly father, Joseph, and He loved us all, His brothers and sisters under the Fatherhood of God who created us all.

Could He, Who died on the Cross for all humanity, have so loved the people of the world if He had not loved those who were nearest to Him?

Ponder this a minute because in that truth we find another clue to His life and works during those seemingly unknown eighteen years.

The Holy Family

CHAPTER II

The Family of Jesus

If you will turn to Matthew, you will read;

"And coming into his own country, he taught them in their synagogues, so that they wondered and said: How came this man by this wisdom and these miracles?

"Is not this the carpenter's son. Is not his mother called Mary and his brethren James and Joseph, and Simon, and Jude? And his sisters, are they not all with us? Whence therefore hath he all these things?"

There are some who believe from these words that Christ had brothers and sisters. But we shall prove to you that that is not true.

Jesus was the only child of Joseph and Mary; Joseph was not His father in the natural sense for Christ as man was the Son of God by the power of the Holy Ghost. It was necessary that Mary should have a husband and protector, for the time had not come when the whole mystery could be revealed. Christ was too tender towards His mother to have her name used by slanderous tongues as it would have been had the child only possessed an Invisible Father. At first Joseph was reluctant to marry because he had vowed himself to virginity. But when the truth was made known to him by an angel, he accepted the trust. An edict had gone forth that a suitor was to be chosen for Mary and the young men of suitable birth must present themselves for that purpose.

When the suitors were assembled before the High Priest that he might choose a spouse for Mary, Joseph presented himself according to orders. His rod blossomed and that was the sign which proved that he had been chosen by God.

Mary, too, had taken the solemn vow. Her words to the angel of the Annunciation were, "How shall this be done when I know not man?" And the angel responded . . . "The power of the Most High shall overshadow thee."

Matthew tells us: "But while he (Joseph) thought on these things, behold the angel of the Lord appeared to him in his sleep, saying: "Joseph, son of David, fear not to take unto thee Mary, thy wife, for that which is conceived in her is of the Holy Ghost." "For Joseph, before they came together, knew that she was to have a child and, being a just man, and not willing publicly to expose her, was minded to put her away privately."

While the Scriptures tell us little of Joseph, we may build up a picture of him from sayings like these. He was tender toward the little maid he espoused and would not have her reputation soiled; he was kindly as well as just.

Later on in the same chapter of Matthew (I): "Now all this was done that it might be fulfilled which the Lord spoke by the prophet saying:

"Behold a virgin shall be with child, and bring forth a son, and they shall call his name Emmanuel; which, being interpreted is, God with us.

"And Joseph rising up from sleep, did as the angel of the Lord had commanded him, and took unto him his wife.

"And he knew her not till she had brought forth her first-born son; and he called his name Jesus."

The term **first-born** was the title given to the first child at that time whether other children followed or not. The eldest son was of great importance in those days being the inheritor of the tradition and possessions from his father. So the title first-born meant, simply, the important child, whether he had brothers and sisters or was an only child. It also emphasizes the fact that Mary was a virgin when He was born.

The Scriptures affirm that she was His mother; therefore, if he was her "first-born" she had always been a virgin, as she remained to the end of her life.

The great doctor, Jerome, proves by examples from the Scripture that an **only begotten** son was also called **first-born** or **first-begotten**; because, according to the law, the **first-born** males were to be consecrated to God. **"Sanctify to me, saith the Lord, every first-born** . . . among the children of Israel." And the words "till she had brought forth" did not imply that Mary had other children **after** Jesus Christ. This was a manner of speaking among the Hebrews, as Jerome points out by many examples, to denote only **what is done,** without any regard for the future. This quotation from Scripture proves that use: "God saith to His divine Son: **Sit on my right Hand TILL I make thy enemies thy footstool."** Does that mean that He will sit there no longer after His enemies are conquered? But we know that He will sit there through all eternity.

Both Mary and Joseph had made a solemn vow to God of virginity. Would they, close to the Incarnate God, break that vow? Some writers claim that Joseph was a widower with several children when he espoused Mary.

The High Priest summoned only the unmarried men when a spouse was chosen for Mary. The Bible, always definite, would have added, "a widower, the father of several children," had it been true. Surely the Scriptures would have told us of these apocryphal sons and daughters of Joseph, for the other relatives of Jesus are spoken of frequently.

And reason rebels at the thought of the mother and foster-father of **God made Man**, being the parent or parents of earthly children. Theirs was the highest destiny that man and woman

THE CHRIST-BOY LEARNS THE CARPENTER'S TRADE.—From the Painting by Carrache.

ever had. Who could be worthy to be even half-sisters or brothers, in the earthly sense, of Christ? He is spoken of as "the son of the carpenter," not "one of the sons" or even as "one of the children," and, because the man of the family was the important person, not the wife—for the woman's position at that time was subservient—Joseph's offspring would certainly have been mentioned. Yet always Jesus is called, "the son of the carpenter."

There is no mention made in any account of the Nativity of Christ of other members of Joseph's family who would have gone to be enrolled at Bethlehem, the City of David.

Joseph, and Mary too, was of the house and family of David. His sons and daughters, if he had had any, would have been obliged to enroll in the same city. Would they not have been with their father? For a family was enrolled together. Joseph, as the father, had authority over his children. Would he, had he daughters or even daughters-in-law, have allowed Mary to go through her ordeal with no other woman near?

29

Yet we know that there was no one with Joseph and Mary. So we may dismiss the idea that the man who had the sacred trust of watching over the Infant God had other children at that time or at any other time.

The Scriptures, according to the use at the time, call Christ's relatives His "brethren;" James and John, Simon and Jude. **Brethren** meant a close relative; similar to "of the house of, (David)." Paul, in his **Letters to the Romans**, addressed the Romans as "brethren;" adopted brothers in Christ. "Sisters" had the same meaning. Families were closely knit in those days.

Cousins were regarded almost as brothers and sisters; and when a man said "my brethren," he meant those closely related to him or associated with him. And why would Christ, if He had brothers and sisters, leave His (and their) mother as a charge to a comparative stranger at His death? He gave her to John in those touching words on the Cross: "Behold thy mother." John, so Luke tells us, was the son of Zebedee and the brother of James, both being partners of Simon (afterwards Peter); and these three were among the first of the Apostles.

Mark says the same thing; "And going on from thence a little farther, he saw James the son of Zebedee and John, his brother . . . And forthwith he called them. And leaving their father Zebedee in the ship . . . they followed him." So James and John, spoken of as **brethren,** could not have been the sons of Joseph. Nor of Mary, even if it were possible to think that she would marry again after the death of Jo-

THE MADONNA, JESUS, AND JOHN THE BAPTIST.— Painting by Raphael

seph. We know that Joseph was alive when the Child was twelve and He began His life in public at the age of thirty. Suppose Joseph had died when Christ was fifteen, which is putting it at an early age, and His mother had married again. Then the oldest child of that suppositious marriage could not be more than fourteen when He was thirty. So the Apostles, who were close to His age (Peter being much older according to tradition), could not have been real brothers to Christ.

Mark speaks of the morning of the Resurrection when Mary, **the mother of James,** went with Mary Magdalen to the tomb. This was Mary of Cleophas supposed to be a cousin of Mary, the mother of Christ.

James and John were the sons of Zebedee. Jude was the son of Alpheus, the brother of Joseph, the foster-father of Christ. Therefore, they were cousins and "brethren" in the meaning of the word in those times. The tribes regarded their members as one family. So we may confidently regard ourselves as the only brothers and sisters of Christ. "For whosoever shall do the will of my Father that is in heaven, he is my brother and sister . . ."

As an only child, Christ was not without companionship. There were the other children of Nazareth to play with in the village streets and in the fields and woods. His little cousins, perhaps, visited Him and joined in His childish games. We may picture Him, in imagination, with the innocence of all childhood in His bright candid eyes, His reddish brown curls blowing in the wind, dressed in the seamless robe which His mother had woven. Perhaps He is tossing a ball to His cousin James; perhaps He has gathered a group of other children about Him while He recounts some story of the Old Testament, which Joseph has told Him, while the other children listen eagerly.

"My Son, it is time for Thy supper:" Mary calls from the door of the little house set into the side of the hill. The Child instantly obeys. "He went down to Nazareth and was subject to them." He turns at the door to smile once more upon His companions, the children, for always He smiles upon children; "Suffer the little ones to come unto Me, For of such is the Kingdom of Heaven."

Christ perhaps, never saw His cousin, John the Baptist, unless when they were babies, for John went, while still young, into the desert, and they did not meet until Christ came to John to be baptized. Yet because Mary and Elizabeth, the mother of John, were so devoted to each other, perhaps the two mothers made visits with their little sons. The Early Italian painters have given us many such groups, chiefly of Mary and the two children.

John, the cousin of Christ, was His precursor; the forerunner of the "One Who was to come." John's mother knew the great secret when Mary visited her just before John was born." "And whence is this to me that the mother of my Lord should come to me?" John could not remain at home for many years. His work of preaching and baptizing called him away. The families lived far apart, so, we suppose, the two parted when they were children, not to meet again until that great day when Christ sought John in the desert.

The idea of earthly brothers and sisters of Christ seems to have sprung from the thoughts of agnostics—those who would deny all thought of the Divinity of Christ. To prove that He is Divine, we have the words of God the Father, Himself, at the Baptism. "Thou art My Beloved Son in Whom I am well pleased."

AND ALL THAT HEARD HIM WERE ASTONISHED.
—Luke II, 47

CHRIST AND THE FISHERMEN

CHAPTER III
The Family at Nazareth

The hidden life was lived at Nazareth in the home to which Joseph had brought Mary from Egypt. Christ lived there with his mother even after the death of Joseph which occurred sometime between the visit to the Temple when Christ was twelve and the beginning of His public life, about the age of thirty.

Joseph was a carpenter and plied his trade in the village to which he had come, a stranger. He had to make his way and so the family was poor. Mary had to eke out, as many another mother has to do, the pittance which Joseph gave her for the family expenses. Their food was frugal but we may be sure that it was well-prepared and that the small house shone with cleanliness. It raises housework to a new dignity when we remember that Mary, the mother of God, performed her daily round of tasks aided, perhaps, by the little Boy, Himself. As soon as the Boy reached the age of seven, He became the charge of His father, rather than His mother, as was the custom of the time. Joseph began to train his Son in the meaning of the religious laws and also he taught Him his own trade.

The great love which Christ had for His mother is borne out in many passages in Holy Writ. This truth is so well established, it should require no additional testimony.

Nobody in Nazareth suspected that the little house sheltered a family which was different from themselves. True, the Boy was never in mischief, He was perfectly obedient and polite to every one, but that was to be expected of the son of Mary and Joseph who were always quietly courteous and obeyed implicitly all the rules of their religion. And Jesus was friendly; He proved that in His later life He fed the hungry, as we learn from the Miracle of the loaves and fishes. Surely He felt that compassion for suffering all His life. We can imagine Him and His father going quietly under the shelter of a dark night to bring a basket of food to neighbors poorer than themselves. And if some little playmate hurt himself, how quickly would the Divine Child rush to him and console him with loving words! The Family must have lived in their daily life the words uttered by Jesus later on: "Love thy neighbor as thyself." In the true sense, that means all mankind without exception but how well it applied to their immediate neighbors, the lowly people of Nazareth! Perhaps, as He grew older, He gently remonstrated with sinners, urging them to repent; we cannot know this for it has not been written down, but gentleness and kindness and true charity must have marked the actions of the Three.

In order to provide for the home, especially as Joseph grew weaker with age as the Boy advanced toward manhood, and then after that loving father died, Jesus had to work at a trade which was profitable in a small degree and which was honorable — one which all men might see. It was the custom of the Jews to teach trades to their sons so that they would at all times be self-supporting.

Suffer Little Children to Come Unto Me

CHAPTER IV

Jesus, the Worker in Wood

Justin Martyr (100-150 A.D.) says that Jesus was known to be a worker in wood. This may have placed Him as a cabinet-maker as well as a carpenter and there is no reason that He could not have been both.

He had been brought up in His father's trade; most certainly He followed it and did His work perfectly, as He did everything.

As a carpenter or wood-worker, He would be able to live a quiet life without attracting widespread or unusual attention. He might pursue His meditations and His studies, His prayers to His eternal Father and the planning for His public life in peace. And yet, He led a life such as any ordinary man leads. He was "to show us the way." He worked, He ate, He slept, He walked, He talked with His mother, His friends and neighbors, as we do. Nothing seemed to mark him as different from the other young men, except dignity, kindness and sinlessness.

THE 18 ABSENT YEARS OF JESUS CHRIST

True, as a child, He had displayed unusual wisdom in His talk with the doctors at the Temple.

Perhaps, when He returned home, there was some curiosity and some awe but as the years flowed on and no other like event occurred, it was almost forgotten. He may have taught in the synagogue; perhaps the children flocked to His knees to hear Him explain the Law and the Prophets. He may have foretold the New Law which He was to bring, emphasizing the words which spoke of the Messiah Who was to bring it. But He did not tell them, "I am He Whom the prophets foretold."

In the cool blue evening, as He and His mother sat at the door of their cottage to breathe the cool evening air and to rest after the day's labors, a bevy of little ones may have clustered about His knees, to beg Him to "tell them a story."

Whatever we may picture of those days, we know that He led a life like our own with its daily accumulation of worry and troubles. He felt heat and cold, hunger and thirst. No angels came to wipe His brow as He labored in the hot sun on a neighbor's roof-beams. No seraphim sang Him to sleep as He sank on His hard couch after the day's work. He lived as man and completely as man, that He might be one of us. He knew Who He was, that He was God as well as Man. Simeon, when he circumsized the Child shortly after His birth, had the Truth revealed to him, and also Anna, the Prophetess in the Temple, but no one else knew except His mother and His foster-father, and Elizabeth and her son, John the Baptist, the Precursor. Christ was thirty before His Father sent Him out on His Mission.

After the age of twelve, Holy Writ has nothing to say of Him until His public life began. He lived as a simple villager. There is nothing that we really have to know about that period but we can reconstruct at least the outline of it.

For eighteen years, boy and man, He was preparing for His mission to man. Philosophers have said that "work well done is prayer." Man in general must "earn his bread by the sweat of his brow." Christ did not ask to be exempt from that common lot. He wanted to live as every ordinary man must live. As a skilled and dutiful artisan and as a loving son and neighbor, Jesus was using those qualities which were to flame forth as the most outstanding characteristics of human history.

He experienced the everyday world about Him and repeated His impressions in word-pictures; the sower sowing his seed, the shepherd seeking the lost lamb; they are all there in the Parables.

Whether in His home or in His shop, there were many duties and while attending to them He grew in wisdom and in stature; He became a man and so great was the work which He was to do that He did not leave that home and that preparation until the mature age of thirty.

The law of nature is a law of preparation and growth. Man must follow this law the same as plants and other forms of life.

CHAPTER V
The Bond of Mother Love

We will now regard Jesus Christ, not simply as a man, but as a Being whose parentage was mingled between Heaven and earth.

We cannot regard Him in any other way. Were He not God as well as Man, His purpose could not be fulfilled.

Mary, the mother, must have loved God beyond any conception of the meaning of the word today. Being virgin, she was impregnated with the life-principle direct from the Deity. Beyond other mothers she had devotion to her "first-born," in whom she saw the mighty mission ahead of Him.

We must not for a moment overlook the truth that human and Divine were here united in one Being, and that faithfulness to God called for trust and love and ministrations to man. Nothing could be overlooked. The Child must be trained by her loving care. We can imagine her delight when, holding tight to her hand, the little Jesus took His first steps — her joy when the sacred word, "Mother," came first from His baby lips. That He never gave her a moment's

45

sorrow, except when she reflected on the Prophecies, we can firmly believe, although when He had been left behind at the Temple, when He was twelve years of age and His father and mother "sought Him sorrowing," she was sorely distressed. But a higher call had sounded; He had to be "about His Father's business." Mary understood and reproached Him no further. There was the deepest love between Son and mother and yet we hear nothing of her, after the marriage at Cana — His first miracle which he performed at her request—until we find her on the dolorous Way of the Cross. It must have been a sad parting as He left His home to go out and wander from place to place seeking the souls of man. He fared forth with no money to pay his way, no provision for the future and yet she knew that He must go. "The birds of the air have nests and the fox a hole yet the Son of Man hath nowhere to lay His head." And yet she waved Him a brave farewell before turning back into the home which was to see Him no more— never again.

CHAPTER VI

Christ's Power of Healing

"The Great Physician" was the most marvelous healer ever known. He is the healer of our souls, sick with sin, as well as, in some cases, of our bodies. God has given us natural means for curing disease, herbs and oils, scientific learning of doctors and nurses and we have countless ways of learning how to keep our bodies fit; sensible eating, exercise, cleanliness and other means.

Christ, in His public life, healed many; that was to prove that He had the power of God, although He was also a man. And He gave the power to heal to some mortals, The Holy Ghost descended upon the Apostles and on them various gifts, including that of healing. Others, too, have had that gift but always it comes directly from God.

We shall not go over the many instances of healing which Christ performed. He cured lepers, gave sight to the blind, restored to health those sick of the palsy and raised the dead to life. These and many other wonders He performed in addition to other miracles; and there were perhaps others which are not recorded.

Christ, as man, called on the Third Person of the God-head, the Holy Ghost, frequently, when he performed His miracles. That was so that we, too, when we want inspiration, will ask for aid from the Holy Spirit. He, Himself, became man, "by the power of the Holy Ghost."

Yet, because man finds it hard to believe unless he sees, God has performed miracles, through human agencies. It is a gift rarely bestowed and the recipient is always a very holy person. It is granted only after long and earnest prayer, often accompanied by fasts and penances.

Miracles sometimes come directly from God to the person addressing Him in prayer. Eddie Rickenbacker and his associates on the rafts, testify to this.

And these miracles have not been only of the body but of the soul which is more important. Sick souls have been healed of the disease of sin by the prayers and works of good people. They will have eternal health which is of more importance than the temporal well-being of this earth.

And when there is a healing of the body by the Divine intervention, it must be proved as the miracles at Lourdes are proved. The Jew, Werfel, in his best-seller, **The Song of Berna-dette,** attests to this. The miracles are not called so until the patient who has seemingly been cured has been examined by doctors, and some of these doctors are atheists. All patients are examined before asking for the cure, and afterwards, and then a year must pass. At the end of the year, they are examined again by the medical board and if the ailment has not returned, the cure is declared a miracle. It is God Himself who performs the miracle and not the mother of His Son; it is her intercession that is asked by the pilgrims. We have seen how Christ loved that mother; will His love be any the less, now that they are both in their Heavenly Home, than it was in the humble dwelling at Nazareth?

The Apostles, too, were given the power to heal by the power of God. These wonders attested to the truth which they were preaching. They converted thousands to the startling truths of Christianity.

Very holy people have throughout history, always by calling on Christ and the Holy Spirit, been able to perform miracles. They must be proved by reliable witnesses before we can believe in them. Human nature is credulous but as Tennyson says, "More things are wrought by prayer than this world dreams of."

Usually when a miracle occurs, it has a far-reaching effect; to show the power of God and the truth of God and thus to bring unbelievers to that truth. If we pray earnestly to be cured and God does not grant our prayer, it does not mean that He has not listened to us. There is some Divine reason for it. His only Son called to Him from Gethsemane: "Father, if it be possible, remove this cup from me!" And yet Christ had to suffer pain, humiliation and death. And we know the reason why.

God's justice must be satisfied for the sin of Adam and all our sins. Christ offered us a perfect example that we, in turn, might submit ourselves to whatever is the Will of God. Christ had to suffer that we might be redeemed.

To those who are given the gift of healing, much is demanded; they suffer like unto their "Master"; they devote their lives to prayer and good works; they abjure sin and worldly goods and follow in His footsteps.

Patrick of Ireland is reported to have healed the blind and the sick and the lame. There are tales which have come down to us written down by his contemporaries. Patrick lived only to spread the Word of God and suffered much, body and soul. God does not give this precious gift lightly.

Bernard of Clairvaux, so chroniclers of the time tell us, performed many miracles. He gave

up everything, for he was born the eldest son
of a wealthy noble of the time, and devoted
himself to prayer, fasting and good works. He
gave himself entirely to God and God, in return,
worked many cures of souls and bodies through
him.

To quote the poet, "God moves in a mysterious way His wonders to perform." We all know
of many cases of answered prayer, not achieved
through another human being, but coming direct
to us from God, Himself. The boys who were
adrift on the raft in World War II for weeks
without food, never gave up hope or faith but
prayed constantly. They were rescued and attested to the truth, that God alone had saved
them and that their constant prayer with faith
had kept their spirit alive.

"There are no atheists in fox-holes," laconic-
ally remarked one of the officers at Bataan.

The people whom Christ healed were around
in the streets of the villages and others could
see them and talk to them; thus we are sure

that the cure was lasting and not temporary. There is a form of hysteria where people can believe that they have been cured but this, of course, is not lasting. And we all know of the "will to live" which has kept patients alive. But, in those cases, the disease is conquerable by natural means; the effort of the patient to co-operate is only one reason for his life being saved.

Christ always had dormant power; He was God and nothing was impossible to Him. But He preferred to live an ordinary life during those eighteen years. As man he studied and pondered and observed the life about him and the devious ways of man. He **planned** his career — so important a career—the most important that has ever been on this earth—and it took eighteen years to do so. Surely he does not extend His power lightly or to the unworthy! If we want to be cured, we must go to Him and "pray, pray unceasingly" and, if we do not see that prayer answered, be content to say as He did, "Thy Will be done."

"BEHOLD, I STAND AT THE DOOR, AND KNOCK."

CHAPTER VII

The Education of Jesus

It is evident that Jesus Christ must be educated as man, according to the standards of the time, in order to impress all classes so that His teachings would bear more weight. The beauty of thought and the presentation of it in the Sermon on the Mount would be classic literature even had there been no Divine message throughout.

With His Divine heritage and with the power given Him by His Father to do all things, yet it was necessary that Christ meet the line of human standards. Otherwise many of the people would misunderstand Him and spurn His teachings.

Let us not forget that Jesus Christ came to save man, to redeem the human race and to promulgate the New Law, in which "peace on earth to men of goodwill" would be the ideal.

As He seemed an itinerant preacher, traveling as He did from town to village, had He been unlettered or less wise, some would not have listened to Him. But He could meet argument with answer in any debate with the high-priests or any intellectual scoffer. He used the words and the terms of the time, as one familiar with the daily speech of the people and with the wisdom of the scholars which had been written down. He was "a man of the people and acquainted with infirmity." He **knew** the people from His daily contact with them for almost thirty years. While a young man at Nazareth, doubtless He had walked to the towns in the surrounding country and talked with the elders there and spoken to the villagers. He saw many types of men and women and knew their problems and hardships. Perhaps He advised them in His gentle unobtrusive way with no hint that He possessed Divine wisdom. The children, we know, followed Him, for children, both then and now, loved Him. And He loved the children, reminding us that "unless ye become as little children ye cannot enter the Kingdom of Heaven."

We remind the reader that those eighteen years of preparation must have been spent in the bosom of a sympathetic family. There were no quarrels to upset His serenity, there was no friction to unnerve Him and distract Him from the even pursuit of His preparation. Hard work there was; hard even for a strong young man such as we learn that Christ was. Had he not been physically strong He could not, in His human body, have lived through the flagellation, the tortuous Way of the Cross and the Crucifixion. And, weakened as He was by the sweat of blood the night before in the Garden of Olives, that body would have succumbed before it did on the Cross, had Christ been a weakling. His human mind was clear, His nerves were sound; He had lived a healthy life in every sense. Poor, indeed, in the world's goods but rich in the love of His mother and His foster-father, His friends and neighbors and His relatives. His mother's

cousin, Mary of Cleophas, stood with that Mother at the foot of the Cross; how much affection and amity that implied, for the death in the eyes of all was disgraceful like that of a common criminal! Mary of Cleophas must have loved her cousin's Son deeply to have forgotten everything else except that His mother needed her. Repentant sinners have their prototype in the figure of Magdalen with the other two Mary's.

And Mary of Cleophas, "the other Mary," witnessed the empty tomb immediately after the Resurrection. We might assume that she had gone with St. John when he took the mother of Christ "unto his own" and spent those three days of waiting with her. While the Scripture calls her "Mary's sister," that was, as we have said before, the term of close relationship. There would hardly be two Marys in one immediate family for there was a wealth of Scriptural names to call upon. The word "brethren," which is the masculine of "sisters," is used in Genesis XIII 8, XXIX 15, for the relationship between

Abraham and Lot, Laban and Jacob, and yet we know that they are uncle and nephews, not "brothers" as we use the word.

Mary, the mother of Christ, was the child of Joachim and Anne, who were both far advanced in age and she was their first-born; and it is impossible to believe that Anne had any more children after this miracle-child.

"And there were many women from afar off who had followed Jesus from Galilee, ministering unto Him. Among whom was Mary Magdalen and Mary, the mother of James and John and the mother of the sons of Zebedee." The relatives of Christ had loved Him all His life and John followed Him to the foot of the cross. Because Jude, who was His first-cousin—being the son of Alpheus, the brother of Joseph—deserted Christ at the crucial hour, it did not mean that he did not love Him and had always loved Him. None of the disciples had the sublime courage of Christ, even in His human nature. Their love could not rise above their human weakness. They fled, leaving Him to His fate. But afterwards, Jude showed that love by dying to testify the Truth of Christ. He was clubbed to death and his head severed with an axe.

So Christ had many human affections. Would Jude, among others, have given up all to follow Him, his own cousin, if the disciple had not had a strong love for Him and faith in His truth and wisdom?

Jude was not Judas as some people believe. We know nothing of the background of the traitor except that he always loved money and hoped for power. His weakness shows forth the strength of the other disciples and their true love for the Master. Yet no one loved or understood Christ as did His mother. No other mother, despite all that mother-love means, could ever have understood her own son as Mary understood Jesus. And so, as the world's greatest mother, she had to bear His cross with Him, suffering in sympathy. It is reasonable to think that with such a relationship between mother and Son, there would be no reason which would take Him far from home, even to study, until His time had come.

THE MIRACLE OF CHANGING WATER INTO WINE

THE 18 ABSENT YEARS OF JESUS CHRIST

We now turn to John 19, verses 25, 26, 27.

"Now there stood by the cross of Jesus, His mother and His mother's sister, Mary of Cleophas, and Mary Magdalen. When Jesus therefore had seen His mother and the disciple standing whom He loved, He saith to His mother; Woman behold thy son.

"After that, He saith to the disciple: Behold thy mother. And from that hour the disciple took her to his own."

On the cross, in His last throes of pain, Jesus provided for His beloved mother! She was not the mother of the Godhead, but she was the mother of God for the reason that Christ was God and man in one Person. Her Son did not take His divine nature from her any more than an ordinary man receives his soul from his mother. Do you believe that such a Son could have thought of leaving for any length of time the rooftree of His sacred home those eighteen years before He left it forever to "do His Father's bidding?"

Why, then, should those years cause controversy and discussion? Truly, if we read the facts, we can arrive at a conclusion that defies contradiction.

Many efforts have been made to interpret erroneously the story of Jesus Christ. Many false stories have been constructed out of nothing. But if we study the true records of His actions, His habit of life and His magnificent career—the greatest the world has ever known—we must come to this conclusion that this Son—this Great Son—was the most home-loving of all history. It consecrates all homes where He is loved and served. And yet His love did not end there but spread throughout the world.

We must arrive at the sound conclusion that He, Himself, wished to study, to grow up, to heighten His natural qualities nowhere else than in the home. And, all the time, His mother

knew that He had come to serve the world and
that this little time together would end, seemingly, ingloriously. A mother must let her son
go forth into the world when his time comes.
But never mother was like Mary who knew that
after three years, her Son must die for all men.
Yet the home was peaceful and happy. The
Will of God was the will of Jesus and Mary and
Joseph. They lived their everyday life knowing
that "all these things must be fulfilled," in the
future. They enjoyed the songs of the birds, the
beauty of the landscape, the sweetness of the
flowers; they were happy together and with their
neighbors. The House of Nazareth has always
been the model of a happy home.

THE TOWN OF NAZARETH.

JOHN THE BAPTIST.—From the Painting by Leonardo da Vinci, in the Louvre, Paris.

CHAPTER VIII

Examples of the Necessity of Preparedness

When Jesus Christ was baptized by John and went out to preach and to heal the sick and perform other miracles, He was fully prepared. He did not venture forth as one feeling His way. HE KNEW; for besides the wisdom of His Divine nature, He had been preparing through those hidden eighteen years from His twelfth to His thirtieth year.

Christ seemed to act wholly in a human way to give us an example; "Be ye perfect as your Heavenly Father is perfect." He was baptized to show us that it is necessary although, He, Himself, had no need of it. He obeyed all the Commandments of God to the letter and in the spirit of them. If he was angry, it was a just anger; such as the time He took the lash to the money-changers who had polluted the House of God with their sordid bargainings. And again when he said, "Let him who is without sin cast the first stone," there seems a mild and just indignation in His words accusing the hypocrites. Yet His anger was not a blind rage but a mighty torrent of the loosening of God's justice. To the sinners he was kind even when reproving them. Contrary to the spirit of the times, whose methods of punishment even for slight transgressions were cruel, He declared that the sinner should repent **and live.** To the thief who repented on the cross, He gave the most merciful of all promises: "This day thou shalt be with me in Paradise."

He had met many sinners in the course of His life; even the little village of Nazareth was a small section of the world and a sample of what went on in that world. He knew how to meet the sinners and He knew how to treat them. Sinless Himself, He knew what sin was, not only from His studies of the Old Testament, but from seeing the daily lives of people. His soul was strong from prayer and meditation; He was prepared for His work.

Few men who reach the heights of perfection in their lifework achieve it before their fiftieth

THE 18 ABSENT YEARS OF JESUS CHRIST

year. Our own Abraham Lincoln had many
failures before he became President at fifty-two
years of age. And these men have spent a life-
time of tedious and painstaking labor to attain
their goal.

So the age of thirty, when man is at the height
of his manhood, seems young for Christ to have
begun the work which was to culminate in such
fruitfulness for us all. In the natural sense, even
though He was endowed with keen intelligence
and other gifts, this is not so remarkable when
we realize that all His time was consecrated to
getting ready to convert the world to a new and
a better way of living. Is it unreasonable to believe that He would require the eighteen years,
which also demanded much of His time for labor to support the household of His mother and
Himself, to prepare diligently for that work—
as an ordinary man must prepare himself? He
took on human flesh; He lived the life of humanity with its toils and labors and, as we have
to study to learn, we assume that He, too, hum-
bly applied His mind to learning, to study and
to reflection on the eternal truths.

God the Father sent His Son to be one of us; to act in the ways of mankind. Therefore we assume that "there was no royal road to learning" in His case; however, that learning came easily to Him; He knew, even only in His human nature, what many an old man has not yet mastered. It was in His eighteen years at **home,** amid the peace and understanding and love, that Christ made ready for His work.

His first public miracle was performed because His mother asked it. The wedding-feast at Cana had run short of wine and the Mother asked her Son to help them out. "Woman," He said—which word in those times was an endearment—"What is that to thee and to me?" She knew His high destiny and the unimportance of the success of the feast compared to the salvation of souls. It shows the confidence between mother and Son. But, because she asked it, He changed water into wine. She was so kind that it was a distress to her to see the embarrassment of the bridal couple. She and her Son gave dignity to Marriage by their presence there. At a wedding He performed the first miracle which is recorded. The presence of Christ at the feast shows the sanction of God on the love between husband and wife, which is the first foundation of the home.

"Honor thy father and thy mother," was the fourth of the Commandments given by God to Moses. As man, Jesus was bound to obey these words. Do you believe, therefore, that with this knowledge of His duty, He would have left His parents and gone away from them for eighteen years of His life; that He would leave them while still a boy? His father was much older than His mother and would not be able to work for many years more. Who then would care for her, protect her and support her? That would, indeed, not be "honoring" either her or Joseph. Christ's duty lay at home until He was ready to set out for the three years of preaching and bringing the light throughout the countryside. We may well believe that He was preparing for His Great Mission, and still attending to the needs of His mother and of His father too, as Joseph aged and grew feebler.

The evidence presented here has been of such a nature as any reasoning person can understand.

If we stopped with this and did not point out the great lessons taught by these eighteen diligent years of the Saviour's preparation, we would indeed be remiss.

Christ, having assumed our human weakness, had to have time to develop His knowledge and His wisdom but His mission was so far beyond any other ever in this world, that its spiritual nature is sometimes overlooked or not understood.

We do not print the Sermon on the Mount in whole or otherwise quote fully from the many beauties of Christ's teachings. They are available in the Bible. But we would like to draw from this devotion to His parents and preparation for His work, a few lessons that may be applied by all who would make Him their Example.

CHAPTER IX

To Those Who Would Follow in the Way He Led

Christ had a life before dying on the Cross—a human life. He was man and He was God, the Third Person of the Trinity. And we may imagine that there were times at His workbench, where He deftly plied His trade, when His eyes sought a far region very different from the work-a-day world. It was a hard way that He must tread.

Outside were the sounds of every-day—the prattle of childish voices, the bark of a dog, the clatter of a donkey's hoofs on the stones of the street. There would be washing spread out on the day after the Sabbath and the drone of trades-people with their wares. There would be bargainings and quarrels and disputes.

Also, there would be gossip and spiteful words flung in the heat of anger.

The Master heard these, no doubt, and often acted as a peacemaker; but some rebellious na-

CHRIST ON THE CROSS.—From the Painting by Guido.

tures cannot be conquered by kind words. They hate and keep on hating and out of small hates sometimes there grow large wars. An angry word may lead to bitterness which can be quenched only with blood. Men may not kill for a few pennies, but quarrelling over a small sum may lead to white-hot anger and murder. He knew full well how one small sin may lead to many huge ones. So, when He could not intervene, or when the culprits would not listen to Him, we may imagine the sadness which crept over His loving face. There was nothing in the world He hated except sin. And He was about to die for these men! That was probably the only note of discord which troubled His life in those days of preparation.

Christ was not only the **Shower of the Way** but the Pathfinder and the Trail-blazer. He was sent at the time when so much human history based on hatred and misunderstanding and dire ignorance of spiritual law had formed like a black spider-web over the earth. In the middle was the spider, Satan, trapping all the souls he could lure, offering them money and power and the deceptive pleasures of ugly sins. False prophets arose from time to time, just as they have risen ever since and will continue to rise until they will culminate in the dreadful figure of Anti-Christ.

So Christ found out by human experience, in the grind of daily life as a man among men, what every man must undergo. And He had too, like every fortunate man, a real home as background—with family loves as well as family trials. Perhaps there were dull seasons in the carpenter-trade and there was not enough bread for them to eat. We know that Christ felt the death of His loved ones deeply; did He not weep when He heard that His dear friend, Lazarus, was dead? Think of the time when Joseph fell ill and Jesus and His mother knew that that dear protector would leave them. Joseph had been like a father to Mary as well as to the Child; he was so much older and he knew her high destiny and the respect which an ordinary man feels for his wife was augmented by knowing that Mary was the mother of the God-Man. "Jesus wept." What a glorious death for Joseph, knowing that he had done his work well and being soothed by departing this life with Jesus and Mary at his side!

Yet the little home must have been lonely when that kindly old man had gone to his reward. There was the empty place at the table, there was the listening for a familiar footstep which came no more to the door, there was the deserted tool-box which now the Son must use alone. Neighbors, perhaps, came in to extol the dead man's virtues, making the loss even keener as tales were told of his kindness which even the mother and Son did not know. Yes, Jesus felt human grief in His human nature, He did not try to avoid any experience of the common lot except that which would displease His Father in Heaven—sin. He and His mother were exempt from the curse which Adam transmitted to all his descendents.

The lessons which Christ taught were based on knowledge and keen observation. Man must depend on actualities if he is to deal in realities.

Jesus condemned crime, all forms of felony, selfishness, infidelity, profiteering, all forms of dishonesty, and upheld that which is just and right—justice and goodness which are attainable by all humanity.

There were things which He saw in Jerusalem when He went there every year with His parents for the Passover, in Nazareth, in Capharnum and in other towns and villages nearby.

He knew that what occurs in great cities is but a multiplication of the sins and crimes of villages and country-side and farms.

And He knew that the most desirable attainment is one day to reach Heaven. He suffered anguish when He saw men and women barter their souls for fleeting pleasures or dishonest gains. He knew that all these temporal things must pass away. There is pathos in the thought that having come to earth to bring us everlasting peace just because He loved us, He saw so many throwing away their future happiness so lightly. He knew that there is no happiness compared to the happiness in Heaven. He spared no words to tell us about it and His rejoicing was great when the seed fell "on the good ground" . . . "they who in a good and perfect heart, hearing the word, keep it and bring forth fruit in patience."

"Blessed are the poor in spirit; for theirs is the Kingdom of Heaven."

He was poor and had been poor since His birth in a manger. He had worked for every bite of bread since He was a child. He blessed poverty by His acceptance of it. But the poor **in spirit** means the humble of heart; those whose spirit is not set on riches. Rich men who do nót live for their riches, who use their possessions to help others, who do not glory in their wealth but use it as a stepping-stone to higher things can be "poor in spirit" but theirs is a difficult way. And poor men of rebellious and haughty spirit do not follow the Way of Christ. Envy and hatred have no part in the "poor in spirit." He accepted His poverty gladly as an example to us; as He said, "It is easier for a camel to pass through the eye of a needle than for a rich man to enter the Kingdom of Heaven." Riches blind the eyes of the spirit. Christ wanted to be numbered among the poor and the lowly. "Blessed are the meek for they shall possess the land."

He was meek and lowly. He was humble. The only greatness in His eyes was the Greatness of God. The promised land which the meek will inherit is not an earthly paradise but a heavenly one. And they will possess their souls in peace. They will not be like the wedding-guest who took the first place at the table and was put down because another greater than he, came to the feast. "Friend, go up higher!" The meek are precious in God's eyes. Pride and assertiveness are attributes of Satan. Christ was the personification of meekness in the hands of His enemies during the dreadful days of the Crucifixion. "Father, forgive them for they know not what they do!" Was ever a speech so fraught with gentleness and forebearance? He knew that He had only to ask and His "Father would send twenty legions of angels!" He had only to lift His hand and His persecutors would fall dead at His feet. But "all this was done that the Scriptures might be fulfilled." That sublime forgiveness of the most terrible suffering and vilification by His enemies is not parallelled on earth. Truly He loved even His enemies with an overwhelming love. He knew that Judas had betrayed Him yet he accepted the traitor's kiss meekly; He was meek before Pilate and meek in the hands of the soldiers. And He has inherited, as Man, the Land of Heaven, where He reigns there and over the whole world as Christ the King.

"Blessed are they that mourn for they shall be comforted." Truly, this lifts our tears to a holy height! As we have noticed before, He Himself knew what it was to feel grief. He has been called, The Man of Sorrows, and His mother, the Lady of Sorrows. His parting with His beloved mother, when He went forth from Nazareth, must have been a sore grief to them both. But their souls were strong with the grace of God. Their mourning was deep but one day they would be re-united. It was on the Way of the Cross where they met again and Mary's grief was abysmal. And He grieved for her as any son grieves when his mother suffers. But now their mourning has turned into joy and they are comforted just as those of the rest of us who mourn will one day receive Divine comfort.

Christ's mother knew supreme grief and the day came when she received supreme comfort. Christ's disciples mourned His death and grieved that they had deserted Him in His hour of trial.

"And going out, Peter wept bitterly." They did not know then that He would return to them after His death, coming through closed doors and standing before them in His natural body that had risen from the sepulchre. His natural body really died; His divine soul left that body but returned to it for the Resurrection. They knew He was dead and they grieved. They were sorry, too, when He left them again after the forty days, but they were comforted for they knew that they would meet Him again in His Heavenly Kingdom.

"Blessed are the merciful for they shall obtain mercy."

He was merciful to all living things. Man's inhumanity to man and to the lower creatures is contrary to mercy. The vicious and cruel who hurt and abuse wantonly, even in secret, can hardly plead for mercy for themselves when their final account is rendered before the Justice-seat. God knows all things, even our secret thoughts and actions. As we hope for mercy, we must be merciful. **Might** is not **right** and those who practice that philosophy often receive their deserts even in this world.

"Blessed are the clean of heart for they shall see God."

Of all men, Christ was purest of heart. Nothing that this world could give would tempt Him; not even the promise of Satan to make Him ruler of all the earth and its riches. Christ as man could be tempted. Temptation to sin does not mean sin; the will may resist and be stronger than before. Satan approached Christ when His body was weak from fasting in the desert. Satan had seen many fall, when pleasure or power was offered them. So he tempted Christ even believing, in his pride, that he could make Him fall down and adore him. Christ was hungry. Satan tempted Him and taunted Him: "If thou be the Son of God, command that these stones be made bread!" Christ could have turned the stones into bread easily, as He turned water into wine, and quenched His hunger; it would have been sinless in itself, for He had the power from God. But He would not obey even a suggestion of Satan. Christ exemplified completely His own rule: "Thou shalt love thy God with thy whole mind and thy whole heart and thy whole strength," which He followed with the gracious promise: "This do and thou shalt live." You shall live forever as He lives forever and ever in happiness and joy. One reason for His great love for little children was that they are innocent and clean of heart.

"Blessed are they that suffer persecution for justice' sake; for theirs is the Kingdom of Heaven."

He was the most persecuted of all men—the most maligned—the most misunderstood.

If He were to come back to earth, poor and humble as He was then, and preach the straight way, would we who so passionately claim fealty to Him receive Him? Or would we deny Him? We have seen, almost since the beginning of this century, persecutions as bad as in the old Roman times. People have been driven from their homes, families have been separated, the men of God have been tortured and imprisoned. Many of them have thus suffered because they would not forswear their God and adopt the god of materialism—the god of the pagans. And all suffered because of the satanic greed for power and possessions of evil men. The persecuted receive our pity and our prayers and material help and we know that their suffering was not in vain for God will one day compensate them.

Yet whose suffering can compare to that of the gentle Christ? He had every torture of mind and body. He suffered for our sins as atonement to God for us; He suffered for justice' sake. The Kingdom of Heaven was His always and always will be, yet He endured persecution without a protest, giving us the advice which He, Himself, followed to the letter:

"Love your enemies; do good to them that

hate you; and pray for them that persecute and calumniate you."

"Blessed are the peacemakers; for they shall be called the children of God."

What a sorry mess the world has found itself in, time and time again, and how the peacemakers have been scorned! The angels sang at His birth, "Peace on earth to men of goodwill." Men of goodwill have peace of heart, fundamentally, no matter how many disturbances overlay it. **Peace** is a word beautiful in sound as well as in meaning. No other joy on earth can compare to it. We have all suffered everywhere because of the warlike spirit which has taken possession of the earth. We have had to fight that one day we may achieve peace. Yet not only nations need peace. Neighbor quarrels with neighbor; children are encouraged to battle over their small wrongs. The air rings with shrieks of dissension. Few are the peacemakers to cast a placating word into broils. We have seen how Christ had peace in His home and brought peace

87

whenever He walked abroad. An understanding word, a little joke perhaps, a calm request to talk the matter over quietly, will sometimes settle a matter which otherwise would spread and grow more serious with time.

There are too many trouble-makers who enjoy dissensions. They will whisper "what so-and-so said about you," and carry the tale of a heated reply back to the sayer. They are quick to imagine evil of what is, perhaps, an innocent action and spread the result abroad. They love to live in an atmosphere of scandal, of bickerings and fighting.

Few are the peacemakers; the people who recount the pleasant words one man has said of another; those who, when they see trouble beginning, smooth it over with kindly words. A truly strong man loves peace; it is the weakling who harries himself and others.

In times of peace, the home is happy. Flowers grow and children run and play and laugh.

Grown-ups see the results of their plans, and works bear fruit. Art and learning, science and achievement flourish. And those who make and keep peace will be called "the children of God."

The Sermon on the Mount is as vital today as it was the day on which it was preached; the message is eternal—for all times and all peoples. Spoken a little more than nineteen hundred years ago, its message rings down through the ages as an inspiration and pathway for our stumbling feet.

It is said that a great American electrical laboratory has for years been working on a device to reach out into space to try to pick up the vibrations of anything that has ever been said, as science declares that any vibration of the air goes on endlessly.

The objective is to pick up His voice as it preached the Sermon on the Mount!

But are we like Thomas, "of little faith" that we must see to believe?" Or, in this case, to hear? Even were the Beatitudes a human document and not the words of God, they contain wisdom and beauty of thought and language which, if followed, would make this sad and sorry world a foretaste of Paradise.

Throughout eternity that Voice will ring out and tell the Universe the verities of His message: the goodness of God and that we are all His children, being brothers to Christ because He took flesh and became one of us, a man like ourselves.

He tells us to love our enemies. We must hate the sin but love the sinner. Hatred has been spread through the world; national hatred and personal hatred. And yet we pray, "Forgive us our trespasses as we forgive those who trespass against us." We must fight the Nazis and the Japanese or be destroyed ourselves. It is a just war. But we may not hate the peoples of those countries for they are our brothers in Christ: He died for them as well as for us.

They have been deceived by false teaching. Might has taken the place of right in those countries. Yet, "he that takes the sword shall perish by the sword." Those false leaders will receive a just punishment and the conquered peoples will be restored to freedom. Then we will, according to the words of Christ, "Feed the hungry and clothe the naked."

"Blessed are the merciful; for they shall obtain mercy."

"Blessed are the peace-makers for they shall be called the children of God."

We have seen that God answers our prayers. We will pray for a just and lasting Peace and being, in that sense, Peacemakers, we will be called "the children of God," with full meaning. In that way we will truly "love thy neighbor."

Christ found earthly love in His home and He brought to it Heavenly love as well. As He spent thirty years there, does not that show the

THE DESCENT FROM THE CROSS.—From the Painting by Rubens.

value He places on the home?

The Family was poor. The home was only a poor little house built into the side of a hill. Yet love and peace and prayer and contentment were there.

Conclusion

The facts have been presented to you. Do you believe that He could have been so understanding in His human qualities, so one of us, without a home here on earth as well as in Heaven?

Do you believe that the One who has done more for humanity than ALL OTHERS COMBINED could have been so like ourselves unless he had lived in a HOME here on earth, with a tender, loving mother and father, and relatives and friends—yes, and enemies!—like an ordinary man?

Were those eighteen years lost? Nothing that Christ ever did was without meaning. They were

THE 18 ABSENT YEARS OF JESUS CHRIST

the preparatory years for the GREATEST OF ALL CAREERS!

For the One who came to save man, lived those eighteen years at home; those busy, vital, beautiful eighteen years of physical growth and preparation.

It is the home which forms the character; if Christ loved His home so much that he spent all but three years of His life with His parents, we can have no better model.

God bless our homes and may we keep them pleasing to Him!

THE END

ALSO AVAILABLE FROM THE BOOK TREE

Lightning Source UK Ltd.
Milton Keynes UK
UKHW011820250419
341617UK00001B/20/P

9 781585 092710